Jogging into Space

Written by
Cath Jones

Illustrated by
Lisa Hunt

It was Monday and Gill and Chris were at Space Club. They were both looking up at the night sky.

"Look!" Gill said. "I can see the lights of a spacecraft. It is orbiting our planet."

"Space starts about sixty miles up in the sky," she whispered. "I read that in a book."

"No way!" Chris replied.

"Gill's right," their teacher told him.

"I want to go into space," said Gill.

On Tuesday, their teacher told them they should all do something to get funds for charity.

They would need to find sponsors.

"I'm going to ride my bike a long way," Chris said. "What about you?"

"I'm going to travel into space!" said Gill. "I'm going to jog sixty miles. I'll go round and round the school grounds until I've reached space!"

"Wow!" was all Chris said.

On Wednesday, Gill set off on her sponsored jog. Her dad came with her for the first part.

Each day, she would jog part of the way into space.

Would she make it to space? She was not very fast and her jogging was a bit jerky.

It began to rain, but Gill kept on going.

"I'm going to be a success," she told herself.

On Saturday, when Gill looked out of the window, it was snowing!

"Snow!" Dad said. "Jogging to space is going to be a bit tricky."

"I'll take it slow," she told him. "I have to get to space."

Gill's feet hurt.

"Why don't you stop?" Chris asked her.

"No!" Gill cried.

That afternoon, Chris and a whole group of people from school joined Gill on the jog into space.

A band played music too. Then a reporter turned up!

The next day, six people in space outfits hopped out of a coach.

"We've come to join you," they told Gill.

"Buzz!" Gill cried. "I thought you were on that spacecraft I saw in space, last week!"

Buzz was an important astronaut.

"I depart for space on Saturday!" Buzz said.

Jogging in space outfits was slow and jerky. Gill kept up with them, no problem!

A week later, it was the last day of Gill's jog into space. Today she would finish her sixty mile jog!

The whole school joined in with her for her last day. The teacher put up a huge screen too.

As Gill crossed the finish line, the huge screen flickered into life.

"Welcome to space!" said Buzz, from his spacecraft.